© 1993 Emma Books Limited.
Published by Emma Books Ltd., Beckington, Somerset, U.K.
Designed and produced for Selectabook Ltd., Devizes, Wiltshire.
Illustrated by Miranda Gray. Printed in Italy.

Ponds and Streams

Words by Janine Amos
Pictures by Miranda Gray

① Frog

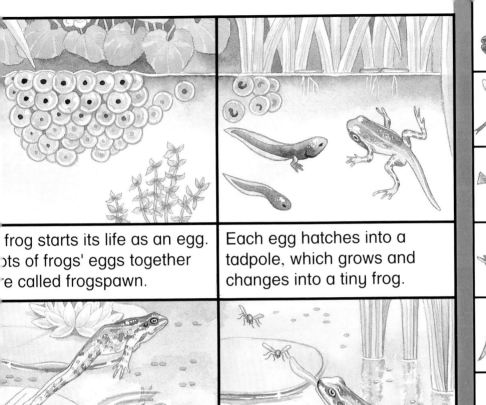

A frog starts its life as an egg.
Lots of frogs' eggs together
are called frogspawn.

Each egg hatches into a
tadpole, which grows and
changes into a tiny frog.

Frogs use their strong back
legs for jumping and
swimming.

Frogs like to eat flies. They
catch them on their long,
sticky tongues.

 ①

 ②

 ③

 ④

 ⑤

 ⑥

 ⑦

 ⑧

② Dragonfly

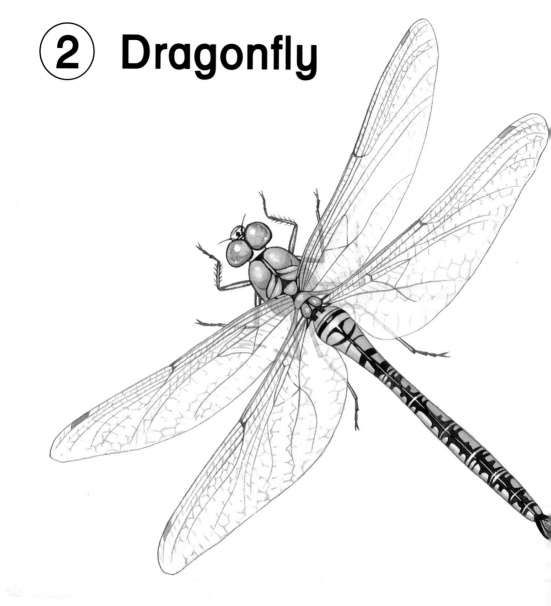

agonflies can fly very fast
d change direction quickly.
ey hunt other insects.

They have big eyes so they
can spot other insects a long
way off.

oung dragonflies (nymphs)
ve no wings. They live
derwater.

Nymphs can climb out of the
water and shed their skins to
become dragonflies.

②

③

④

⑤

⑥

⑦

⑧

③ Stickleback

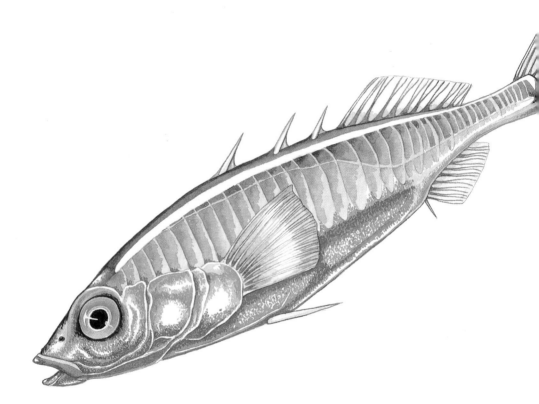

he male stickleback makes
nest, then dances to attract
female.

Sticklebacks are caught by
kingfishers and otters (see
index numbers 6 and 8).

ticklebacks have spines on
eir backs to protect them
om their enemies.

The female lays her eggs in
the nest. The males keep
guard while the babies grow.

③

④

⑤

⑥

⑦

⑧

(4) Mallard

llards have waterproof
thers. They tip upside
wn to find food underwater.

Mallards pair up in spring.
The males show off their
bright feathers.

e female builds her nest in
uiet place, hidden from
w in the reeds.

Ducklings swim and find their
own food, but mother duck
protects them.

④

⑤

⑥

⑦

⑧

(5) Great-crested newt

ewts hide under stones or in eds near water. They come t at night to feed.

In spring, the males grow crests on their backs. Their bright colours attract females.

ewts are amphibious, like gs. This means they can e in water and on the land.

Young newts are called efts. They live in water at first, and then on land.

⑤

⑥

⑦

⑧

(6) Kingfisher

ngfishers search for food in streams. They dive down to catch fish.

They swallow their prey whole (see index 3). They also eat insects.

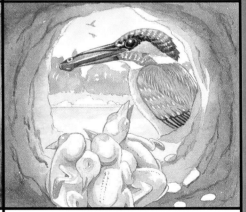

hey nest in a tunnel in the riverbank. The female lays six or seven eggs.

The chicks are born with no feathers. Both parents bring them food.

⑥

⑦

⑧

⑦ Diving beetle

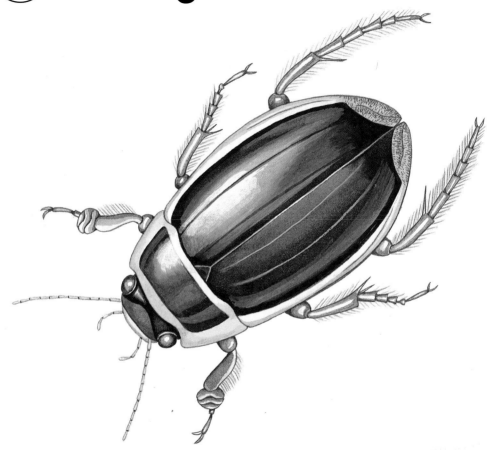

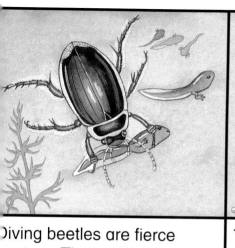

Diving beetles are fierce hunters. They will eat anything they can catch.

They use their hairy, flat legs to paddle along in the water at great speeds.

When under the water they breathe air trapped under their wings.

When they first hatch they have long, soft bodies. They then grow into beetles.

(8) Otter

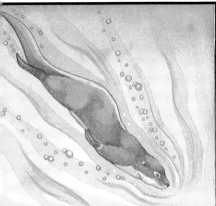

tters swim well. Underwater
ey keep their eyes open,
unting for fish.

They love to play. They even
make slides down the river
banks.

he mother looks after her
ubs in an underground
urrow.

When an ottter catches a fish
(see index 3), it takes it
ashore before eating it.